MEMOIRS OF AFRICA

1996 TO 2009

DELORES J. DILLARD

To order additional copies of this book, contact:
Xlibris
1-888-795-4274
www.Xlibris.com
Orders@Xlibris.com

CONTENTS

DEDICATION

This book is dedicated to the family of Mrs. Christiana Darko. Christiana is the one who introduced me to Africa. I met her in Vancouver, Washington in February 1996. She invited me to come to Ghana. I went to Ghana in July 1996. This trip changed my life for all eternity. It opened the door to the rest of Africa for me.

Christiana taught me how to walk in my anointing as a minister. She never compromised her place as a woman of God. She was always a lady. She wore so many different hats. I wouldn't attempt to do all of the things she excelled in. The thing that is so amazing is everything she did was done with compassion and excellence.

The things that stood out most about her are: she loved her God, she loved her family and she had the love of God for all people. Her prayer life made her prosper in every area. Christiana went to be with the Lord, October 7, 2012. I will see her again in heaven. May her family know how much I loved Christiana. I thank each of them for sharing her with the world

Delores(first) Christiana (third) and Women Aglow Friends

Ghana—1996, 1997, 1998, 1999, 2001, 2006, 2008

PASTOR Kwabena & Dr. Christiana Darko

My travels to Africa started in 1996 to Ghana, West Africa. I have been there 7 times. My host family has always been Mr. Kwabena and Mrs. Christiana Darko. Ghana is a nation on the West Coast of Africa. It is one of the most thriving nations on the continent. It is sometimes referred as an "island of peace" in one of the chaotic regions on earth. It is bordered by Togo to the east, Cote d'Ivoire to the west, Burkina Faso to the north and Guinea to the south. The country's economy is dominated by agriculture, which employs about 40 percent of the working population. Ghana is one of the leading exporters of cocoa in the world. Gold and lumber are also significant commodities. The population of Ghana is estimated to be 22 million. Accra is the capitol city. There are more than 100 ethnic groups—each have their own unique language. However, English is the official language due to British colonization. The land area is slightly smaller than Oregon.

CHRISTIANA & DELORES

In 1996 the roads were rocky and underdeveloped. I was amazed to see the streets didn't have traffic lights. The airport was very unorganized. The cede,their local currency, was unstable. On my last visit in 2008 all of this had changed. The roads were paved and a pleasure to drive on. The airport was clean and running smoothly. The biggest shock was the currency. Previously, when I exchanged $200.00 to cedes, I needed a bag to put the money into. When I made the exchange on my last visit; I discovered the value of their currency was almost equal to the U.S. dollar.

Most of our meals consisted of chicken or fish, rice and vegetables. Darko Farms, at that time, was the largest producers of chicken in West Africa. They had a chicken industry that hatched the baby chicks, produced the feed and sold eggs at several outlets. Many restaurants and individuals purchased the products. When my hostess told me they had a farm with a few birds.(chickens) I was overwhelmed to see 200,000birds.

WOMAN WITH CHILD ON BACK

The team for 2001 consisted of 15 people; 9 children age 9-15 were part of the group. A single mother, her 13 year old son and 9 year old daughter were team members. The mother paid her fare and her sons'. Another team member paid the daughters fare. A week before our departure, the mother was laid off of her job and evicted from their apartment. The mother kept moving forward, she said God wanted her family to go. While we were in Ghana the daughter said God had spoken to her. She said she was called to be a missionary. This daughter has gone on several missions trips since that time.

We took the group to visit Elmina Castle. This was one of the castles where slave trading was done. It was a sobering time. The children were very quiet. The guide said, the men slaves were placed in small rooms with no ventilation. The women were placed in different small rooms. Some of the people jumped into the ocean to their death rather than be taken to another nation to be enslaved. Over one of the archways were these words, "the place of no return." After going through the castle, we had to debrief the children. One of the boys said, I don't know why people hate us so much. What have we done to deserve this? We told them man is greedy and wants to dominate.

When God told Adam to rule over the earth, it was never his intention that man rule another man. Man's domination should be over animals and not another human. The slave owner's needed someone to do the labor they didn't want to do. The Africans were cheap labor. Consideration of the separation and Destruction of families wasn't considered. We prayed for the children to release any anger or unforgiveness. We also prayed for peace in the land.

On the door of Elmina Castle, the sign, "the door of no return" has been replaced with, "the door of return". This is referring to the African Americans that are coming to find their history. The Ghanaians want African Americans to come back home and invest and retire.

TEAM OUTSIDE OF SLAVE CASTLE

BURUNDI – 2003, 2004, 2009

Pastor Jeremie Ndayishimiye & Family,
Director of Good Samaritan Ministries in Burundi

Burundi is called the heart of Africa. It's about the size of the state of Maryland. The population of Burundi is 8.07 million people, according to the world book information of 2008. This nation is also listed as one of the poorest nations in the world. It has a very young population with 47 percent aged 14 or younger. Only 3 percent of the population is 65 or older.

On April 29, 1972, there was an outbreak of violence in the south of the country. This continued through the month of August. It is estimated that 200,000-300,000 Hutus were killed from April to September 1972. About 300,000 refugees went to Tanzania.

LADY CARRYING GRASS ON HEAD

MAN MAKING DRUM

In July 2003, my friend Sandi and I went to Burundi for three weeks. The U.S. gave a warning stating no American should go to this nation. There was still fighting between the tribes. The rebels were still refusing to lay down their weapons. Sandi and I believed God was saying we should go anyway. When we arrived at the airport in Burundi, Pastor Jeremie, director of Good Samaritan Ministries in Burundi, and 5 of his children met us. The children gave us large bouquets of tropical flowers. We were taken to their home where Jeannie, the pastor's wife, and one month old Tabitha welcomed us.

They assured us we were safe. The rebels were in the up country. They hadn't been to the capital city, Bujumbura, in three years. You could hear the continuous gun fire in the distance. The next day we started the children's program. Sandi lead the children in soccer games. I was responsible for the Bible story and art project. We had interpreters because we didn't speak their language and most of them didn't speak English. The information was translated in Kurundi, Swahili and French. Some of the children lead the praise and worship. The attendance grew daily.

After one week, we were summoned by the U.S. Embassy. We were told to be ready to evacuate at any time. The Embassy told us to keep them informed where we were at all times. We had to leave the pastor's home and discontinue the children's program because of the rebels. It wasn't safe for us or our host to be out in the open. Sandi and I weren't allowed to leave the gated area where we were now staying. We were awaken early one morning to the rebels shooting outside of our quarters. Sandi and I prayed and believed for God's protection. Each day we went to the café on the premises. The waiter gave us the menu. Everything was written in French. We communicated by pointing to photos. Everyday we had a delicious cube of beef in red sauce. This was placed over some rice. The meal also included some green peas. It was very good. The portion of meat was the ounces the dietician say we are supposed to eat. We laughed and said now we know what 3 ounces looks like. One day we decided we would eat spaghetti instead of our usual meal. When the waiter came with the menu, we pointed to the spaghetti. He went to the kitchen and told us they were out of spaghetti. So we ate our usual meal for the rest of our days there.

After a few days, we were able to continue the children's program. The rebels had returned to the up country. Most of our friends were shocked we hadn't returned to the United States. Jean-Claude said, "I know that we are in your hearts because you remained with us at the risk of your own life." Most of the NGO's (none government offices) had left the nations. This included the United Nations.

Caption: Girls Dancing

Sandi and I knew we were on assignment in Burundi. We were there to intercede for peace in the nation. In October 2003, three months after we returned home, the last rebel group surrendered. The nation was free from the gun shots at least for a season.

In 2004 we went with Pastor Jeremy to plant a church in a new area. We drove for miles with red dirt flying everywhere. It didn't look like there was any habitation where we were going. When we finally arrived, the group on the outside of the building outnumbered those on the inside. The church had bamboo poles around it with an opening to enter. The top was partially covered with some tarp and tin; the floor was red dirt. The people were so elated to have their own facility.

TRUCK OF BANANAS

GRADUATION

BAPTISM

MAN DANCING WITH STRAW

ON HEAD

The African Messenger, November, 2009

Sister D: A True Ambassador

O sister D., Mother Delores, missionary, ambassador, mama Africas . . . these are just a few of the names Mama Delores Dillard has been given, thanks to her unselfish love toward a people she now calls her own; Africans. To some, Africa is a " forsaken" place and to others, a place of tourism and whatever exotic things that people look for in life. But to this servant of God, it is home. "I love the people and they love me. I respect the people and they respect me." Mama Delores has inspired others to go to discover the cradle of humanity, Mama Delores' first trip to Africa was 1996 when she visited Ghana on a missionary trip. Since then, she has visited Burundi, Nigeria, Rwanda, Liberia and Kenya. For such a successful and loving woman, it could have been easier staying in America and enjoy life to the fullest, but "that's not what God wants of me", she says. And although some of these countries were not the easiest of places to visit, Mama Delores cared more about the work of God and the impact of her presence within the community she visited than anything else. "On my last visit, there wasn't a time that we had running water, electricity or food at the same time. We would have one or two, but never all three. But this was a small thing compared to the relationships that were developed." She reflects.

Gloria Ngezaho (Founder/Editor in Chief of "The African Messenger")

Born in Burundi

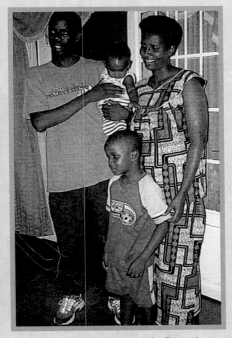

Freddy Tuyizere & Family
Director of Youth
for Christ in Burundi

Delores Dillard is one of the strongest women I have had the priviledge to meet in my entire life. She is strong in character and in faith of the invisible God ;and she is courageous. As I visited her in the U.S., I came to realize she is the same whether she is home or being in a war-zone country like Burundi. I met her when she came to Burundi in 2003 while our country was still in terrible times of war-genocide. I remember a particular moment when the U.S. Embassy in Bujumbura called all of their citizens to be evacuated outside of Burundi because it was very dangerous; but Delores and her friend Sandi didn't leave our country until their mission was accomplished. We felt so loved and supported. After that first visit they came other times to help the children, women and churches in general. In Burundi, we are always encouraged to host Delores and her teams because they always bring messages of hope in our broken society.

One day, I invited her to speak to the Youth for Christ women's group-her speech was just half an hour but it was a turning point for some. Delores is a blessing to many lives including mine. I feel so honored that I can call her mom and friend. I pray that God continues to use her to change many more lives in Africa and the world.

Liberia—2006

Pastor Love & Minister Carter, G.S.M. Counselors

     Liberia is one of the few African nations not colonized by an European country. This nation was founded and colonized by freed American slaves. In 1847, they founded the Republic of Liberia. The capital city was named Monrovia, after James Monroe, the fifth president of the United States. Their flag is red,white and blue. Their currency is called a dollar. Their official language is English. But there are numerous tribal languages. They have many religions including traditional beliefs, Christian and Muslim. About 85% of the population lives below $1.25, U.S. dollars per day. The population of those 0-14 years is 44.1 percent. The ones that are 15-64 is 53%;65 years and over :2.8 percent. Life expectancy at birth is 56.8 years.

When Pastor Tressie and I visited Liberia, we stayed with the director of Good Samaritan Ministries, Lucy Saifa and her 5 children. Lucy gave us her bed and she slept on the floor. We didn't like this arrangement. But this is the way it is. The Africans are very loving people. They offer the best that they have to their guests. The country was still torn because of 15 years of war. You could see replicas of businesses, churches and schools. It was evident that this was nation was once beautiful and thriving. It was also evident that restoration would take some time.

We went to a vocational school where students were training to become electricians, plumbers and tailors. This was unique because the students were former rebels. They were drugged as youth and given weapons to kill their own countrymen. Many of these students looked very sad. I am sure forgetting the past must be difficult for them. Pastor Tressie sang for them and I encouraged them as they prepared for a new life.

Pastor Tressie writes : Delores, Jesus said in St. Mark 16:15, Go ye into all the world and preach the gospel to every creature. Because of your faith in the Lord, you trained us to be missionaries in Africa. It was a pleasure bringing clothing, school supplies and toiletries to the church in Ghana and Liberia. Thank you for taking 9 young people from The International Fellowship Church to Ghana. Our tour of Cape Coast was magnificent. I am forever grateful.

RWANDA – 2004, 2009

Pastor Francis Ntuyahera & Family, Director of G.S.M. in Rwanda

Rwanda is known as the land of a thousand hills. It is located in the Great Lakes region of eastern-central Africa, bordered by Uganda, Burundi, The Democratic Republic of the Congo and Tanzania. It is close to the equator but has a cool climate because of its high elevation. It consists of grassy uplands and hills. It has received international attention due to the 1994 genocide in which 800,000-1,000,000 lost their lives. The genocide had been carefully planned.

Rwanda has traditional courts, called gacaca, which means the small lawn where village elders get together to solve disputes. The gacaca process requires that the people who oversee the process are chosen for their wisdom and integrity.

I visited Rwanda for the first time in 2004. I dreaded going in one sense. The world looked during the genocide but no one came to their rescue. I assumed the nation would be very depressing. But I found a nation full of anticipation for a positive future. The nation was rebuilding after such inhuman actions had occurred. There were high rise hotels, banks and other businesses all over the nation.

One of the places we toured was the genocide museum. Some of the burial plots were on the outside. The bodies were encased in mahogany caskets with silk flowers tied with a large ribbon on top. The caskets were stacked on top of each other. There were about 10 bodies per grave. On the inside of the museum was a plague from William Jefferson Clinton Foundation.

GRAVES AT THE GENOCIDE MUSEUM

The Rwandese loves former President Clinton. In 2004, he was the only American president that had ever visited that nation. Each floor in the museum has a different feature. On the first floor, were photos of various people who were killed. A video played in the background. A survivor talked about the shock of the whole event. She talked about the confusion of neighbors killing one another. She was 32 years old. Both of her parents and all of her siblings were killed in the slayings. She was the lone survivor.

On the next floor were bronze plaques with the faces of children on them. This floor was called "The Missing Children". A biography with information such as: favorite food, color, sport etc. was available. It also gave the weapon that was used to kill the child-gun, machete or strangulation. This helped us know these were real people. On the last floor were other nations that had experienced genocide: Cambodia and Bosnia. Photos of these people were included with the number killed. The outside of the museum was very pretty with flowers on the premises. The atmosphere was pleasant and peaceful.

I returned to Rwanda in 2009 with two other ladies. The nation continues to flourish. We rode a bus to a wedding. The bus was immaculate. The driver stopped several times to remind the passengers that eating wasn't allowed on the bus. No one was allowed to stand up or sat on some ones lap. In some nations in Africa, people and animals are packed into the bus like sardines. You don't have room to move.

The people are so glad to have visitors. Many people are coming to assist in rebuilding the nation. They are hard working people. They are helping to keep their nation clean. They have monthly clean up sessions in the community. Everyone must participate. The government is environmentally aggressive. A law has been passed that prevents usage of plastic bags. You can't bring any into their country.

Pastor Francis and his wife have 6 children. They have two sets of twins and two other children. They believe in the principle of sowing and reaping. After ministering in their church, he insisted that the congregation give us an offering. Some of the congregation didn't move out of their seats. Pastor Francis wouldn't move until they gave. This was very humbling for the team. Each of the team members have their own story of what they did to make the trip.

Pre-school Children

NIGERIA – 2004, 2005

Dr. Faraday & Pastor Angela Iwuchukwu, Director& Assistant G.S.M. Nigeria

Nigeria is about the size of California, Nevada and Arizona. The population for 2010 is listed as152 million. Nigeria is the most populated country in Africa. Over half of West Africa's population lives here. Less than 25% of Nigerians live in urban areas. At least 24 cities have populations of more than 100,000. There are 250 ethnic groups in this nation. The variety of languages, customs and traditions gives the country a diverse heritage.

Clare Person, Delores Cuie, Melody Jackson and I went to Nigeria in 2004. We went through customs in Lagos. There were two men and one lady. The men said we would have to pay more money because of the gifts in our luggage. I told them the items were not for sale. We brought them to give to the children. The lady said, "Welcome to our nation". She told the men these are missionaries. We will not make them pay additional money. She told us to go to our connecting flight. When we left the area, they were loudly discussing the situation. We were glad for the interception of the customs lady. We spent the night in Lagos before continuing to Port Harcourt the following day. We were told at the hotel, a free continental breakfast was included with our rooms. None of us were too excited. We assumed it was the usual toast, juice and coffee. The next morning when we went to eat, to our amazement, there was food fir for a king. There was a variety of fruits, breads, smoked chicken, ham, eggs juice, coffee and tea.We didn't have time to enjoy it. We had to catch our next flight. Now we know, continental breakfast has a different meaning at least in that particular hotel in Africa.

When we arrived in Port Harcourt, we decided to have a fundraiser for the counseling center. Many people in the community didn't know the function of the training center. Both Delores and Melody sang with the locals in a concert. It was a great outreach to the community.

Dr. Faraday Iwuchukwu is the director of the center in Port Harcourt. His wife Pastor Angela is the assistant director. They are blessed with 6 beautiful gifted children. This is one of the most generous families I have ever met. The training center has three floors. When we were there, it wasn't completed. The first floor is the counseling center; second floor is the sleeping accommodations for students and guest; third floor for the host family.

The students who came for training came from Ghana, Liberia, Sierra Leone, Senegal, Cameroon and Togo. This center is the training site for all of West Africa. The students came for two months of intensive training. They will use the tools they have learned in the counseling centers of their particular nation. This is the first time that most of them have ever been away from home. The food, climate, language and clothing are different for each nation. The common ground is their love for Jesus and desire to help their countrymen.

Counseling is a new ministry in Africa. It's still frowned upon in many places. Many Africans don't believe it is necessary to express your feelings. This is also true with African Americans. Exposing your pain and hurt is not acceptable, especially, outside of the family. But these Africans saw the healing that many had experienced and wanted to receive the training. One of the ladies from Cameroon was 7 months pregnant. She came on a boat. It wasn't a luxury cruise. She was in the lower part of the boat. Because it was least expensive. Some of her friends tried to discourage her from taking the trip in her condition. But she convinced her husband she would be okay. She did every assignment the other students did; that included the exercises and cleaning of the facility. A few days before the completion of the training, her baby was born in Nigeria. The baby didn't wait for the graduation. The mother and baby flew home to Cameroon.

The training was done by Dr. Faraday, Pastor Angela, Pastor Steve from Ghana, Pastor George from Cameroon and Clare and I from the U.S. The topics included:

Ministering To The Elderly, Healing The Memories Of The Past ,Teaching Tools, Qualities Of A Good Leader, The Importance Of Prayer and Marriage and Family Counseling. The students are given a test after the conclusion of the training. They are graded on their knowledge of the teaching, class participation and involvement in the cleaning and daily exercise.

I needed to type the test for the students in the training center. A student from Liberia and Cameroon and I took a taxi to an internet café in the city. There was a sign in the café with the cost of the usage of the computer. The employee said the price for the services on the sign was incorrect. He said the cost was twice the amount on the sign.

I asked why did he have the sign with the incorrect fee on it. He couldn't look me in the eye. I told him he is the reason that many people don't trust Nigerians. Many expect the Nigerian to try and get the upper hand. I paid the amount he requested. I wouldn't make a scene. He took advantage of us because he knew all three of us were foreigners.

After completing the typing, we had to get the last bus back to the center. There were lots of people waiting for the bus. We were at the front of the line. When the bus came, the people started pushing and shoving. I could see if we were going to get on the bus. We would have to do it the African way. Lining up and waiting for everyone to go in an orderly manner wasn't happening. When in Rome do like the Romans became when in Africa do like the Africans. All three of us made it on the bus. When we told the story to our host and the other students, they laughed. They couldn't image a 61 year old American doing this. You have to adapt to the culture.

Dr. Faraday is a husband, father attorney, bishop; overseer of several churches and director of G.S.M. Several times as we were driving to our destination, we were detained by the military. The military were asking for their endless "fees". When they see the sticker that indicates a lawyer is in the car, we are told to move on. Dr. Faraday could make lots of money if he would focus on being an attorney. But, he said he is a lawyer for the poor. He serves those who can't afford an attorney. So he and his family aren't living like the wealthy. They are making many sacrifices for the good of mankind.

Pastor Angela is Dr. Faraday's wife. She is a gifted teacher, with a master's degree in education and counseling. One of her books,"Sex in Marriage" is the best book on this subject that I have ever read. She is often called to minister to married couples in counseling and seminars. She is also a powerful intercessor and worshipper. We were usually awakened to Pastor Angela praising, worshipping and crying out to the Lord. Besides, all of this, she is a professional seamstress. She started a sewing school to teach young women this skill. When we were there, four women were in training. They made beautiful outfits for all of us and gifts for our family and friends.

Delores with a group of business women

After the students took the test, we had a children's program for the community. The community children lead the songs and danced with the group. The counselors in training performed by acting out Luke 10:25-37; The Good Samaritan story. The emphasis was placed on "Who Is My Neighbor". After the skit, the children were asked if any wanted to receive Jesus. Most of the children, said yes. The men served the children peanut butter sandwiches and juice. This is unusual in many African nations. Many men consider serving food is a job for a woman. Being a Samaritan crosses the cultural tradition.

Class Room of Students, Teacher & the Team

Dr. Faraday took us to his home village, Mbano. He showed us the trickle where many of the villagers get water. The women and children are usually responsible for getting the water. Many of them start lining up before 5 A.M. with their buckets. The cost for a community well is about $50,000. This would have pipes to lead to all 22 villages. The well will serve between 65,000-75,000 people. The well has to be dug about 425". The tank that holds the water sits upon a platform several feet off of the ground. The need for this well is still present. I am praying for others to assist me in this project.

We had to use various mode of transportation to go to minister. Our host family's car wasn't in good condition. And in any case, it wasn't large enough to carry the host family and the four of us. Sometimes we walked, went on public transportation or one of the local people would accommodate us. Public transportation might be a taxi, bicycle or motor bike. I had the pleasure of riding on motor bikes a couple of times. One of those times it was raining really hard and lighting was flashing. Needless to say, my prayer life increased.

There are so many motor bikes because it is cheaper than a car. The drivers act as if they own the road. They take lots of foolish chances. It's a miracle that more people don't lose their lives. Some of my friends in the U. S. and Nigeria asked me if I was afraid. I told them you can't allow yourself to fear. This is the way of life in Africa. You have to be prepared spiritually, physically and mentally to make the necessary adjustments. Anyone that drives in Nigeria will not have difficulty in New York or any other place in the states. There aren't any lanes in the road. You make your own path. And to make matters more interesting, most streets don't have traffic lights. So everyday on the road could be a death trap. But God protected us wherever we went.

The story of the merchant and the custom agents is reality. But so are hundreds of stories of love, kindness and hospitality. All Nigerians aren't crooked any more than Americans. The publicity about Nigerians is more negative than positive.

Every time I go to Africa, I see how blessed we are in America. We have lots of issues in America. But we also have many reasons to praise God every day. Pastor Angela informed us that one of her members needed to go to the hospital. The lady and her husband had four children. She was ready to deliver the 5th child. No hospital would admit her because she didn't have any money. After several attempts, Pastor Angela told the hospital she would pay the fees. The mother and baby needed blood transfusions. Whoever gave blood also had to pay for HIV test. The lady had to have several transfusions. When she was ready she had a huge bill. She couldn't leave the hospital until all fees were paid. I really don't know how long she remained in the hospital.

The following is a letter from Dr. Faraday:

Beloved Mama Delores,

I am glad that you have written a book on your trips to Africa. As for as I am concerned, you are not only a missionary but a unique and charismatic Christian missionary leader. I traveled with you years ago to the remotest villages like Mbemo, Abakaliki, Igbaroke and Arongwa and other villages. You and your team prayed for a barren woman who is a nurse. You did a symbolic action of giving her baby clothes. Today she is the mother of two sets of twins. Her name is Favour Eduo. You never discriminated against any person, food, dress code or local culture. You severally worshipped, danced, preached and prayed for all. I am still optimistic that you will complete the water project.

We love you so much.
Dr. Faraday Iwuchukwu

KENYA – 2009

Bishop James Opiyo, Continental Director of G.S.M. Africa

Bishop James and his assistant Gorrety met us at the airport. We had another three hour drive to go to Uranga. It will be dark when we arrive. We won't be able to see the scenery because there aren't any street lights. Bishop James is the overseer of over 58 churches. He is the Continental Director of G.S.M. for Africa. The other two team members and I will be staying with Bishop James and Mama Teressa. They were the perfect host and hostess. We had warm water every day for our bath. Even though they had many duties, they made sure we had everything we needed. The facilities consisted of the main house and servant quarters which had two separate rooms. All three of us ladies shared the same room, but had a bed, complete with mosquito net.

In Nigeria there were lots of motor bikes used for transportation. In Kenya, it was bicycles. Both of the bikes were used for personal as well as taxi service. The pastors had on suits and ties and were on bicycles. They were glad to have a bike, because previously they were walking. The bikes were made in Germany or Belgium. They were very sturdy. This is necessary because the roads aren't paved.

The people were so receptive to us. We were free to worship and speak the work of God. Several prepared food for us. One couple said they never thought God would honor them by allowing such prominent people to come to their home. We were humbled again. We didn't realize how much our visit meant to the people.

Delores, Evelyn, Gorrety and Sylvia

Pastor Sylvia Jones spoke to the ladies group about the importance of waiting on God for a mate. The women were encouraged and responded as she spoke. Evangelist Evelyn preached and sang. These ladies were a gift from God to the people. Pastor Jones had gone to Ghana with me the previous year. This was her second trip to Africa. Evelyn had never been out of the U.S., she had many culture shocks. I have training for the team for several months before our departure. Evelyn originally came from Illinois. She said this was her first time seeing a live chicken, cow and goat. She looked at the hole in the ground (our toilet) and said, "I'm not using that". I didn't argue with her. I knew she couldn't wait until she arrived in the states.

One of the highlights of the trip to Kenya was going to the family site of President Barak Obama. We took photos with Grandmother Sarah Obama. We met his aunt and saw the gravesite of his father and grandfather. His grandmother received electricity after Barack became president. Kenya is very proud of President Obama. The people in Siaya have schools, streets, hotels and fruit juices named after their kindred. President Obama has been there several times. He took Michelle there before they were married.

Grandmother Sarah Obama & Mama Delores

Bishop James said, "We thank God for the team that was composed of three wonderful spirit filled women. They were nicknamed the three stones that are strong and can cook a good "meal" (the word of God). The team was busy ministering in G.S.M. centers. The center in Ligega was visited late at night. It was raining so hard the team was soaked as they entered the room. We want to report that the team touched the lives of the Samaritans. This was the first team of Africa Americans that have visited Kenya since the beginning of the Samaritan work in Kenya (1987). There coming gave us a sense of belonging. We felt as one family. The team was a blessing to our work in Kenya. We wished they could have stay longer with us so that we could take them to more of our centers to encourage the people. During their visit we learned one thing: ministry should be a team effort. No preacher or teacher is a complete link between God and people. No individual should think he/she can do everything the apostles did. We must be connected with the job God has given us. It is our earnest prayer for the team to come back to Kenya, soon, so that they can minister to our people. God bless you so much for the support you gave to the team that touched many lives in Kenya and Africa."

Education is very important to many people in Kenya and other nations in Africa. Many of the villages we visited have schools that were started and supported by Good Samaritan Ministries. Some of the schools have students that live on campus. Sometimes the children walk or ride bicycles several miles to go to school. Many children were walking to school when it was very dark outside. There weren't any street lights in this area. Sometimes the children would be in groups others were alone; most wear uniforms. Several of the teachers were former students. They wanted to give back to their community.

High School Students

I love Africa. I love each nation and the people that I have met. Each nation has some sameness and differences. What you see on National Geographic isn't the whole truth. There are some rural areas in Africa. But there are some areas that are more modern than some places in America. Many Americans are shocked to see brick houses in America. They are expecting to see huts. The huts are very few in number. They should be called houses, not huts.

The areas where wild animals roam is also limited. Most Africans have only seen wild animals at the zoo. The nations that have wild game is limited because of killing the animals for recreation. The poaching of the skins and other parts of the animals also exist. Many of the people struggle to feed their families due to lack of employment. Graduates from high school and university many times come to America or Europe. They love their nation but want to use their skills. It is very unusual for the students to have a computer at home. They have to go to a public place to use a computer. Many of their schools don't have any computers. Some have one or two computers for several thousand students. Getting an education is not easy. Teacher strikes are common. The strikes can last months or a year.

As you read my journey to Africa, I hope it will inspire you. May you take the leap of faith to your own journey. You may contact me at ddiL911@aol.com for other information. My next trip in 2014 will be to three other nations in Africa. Life is wonderful!

Printed in the United States
By Bookmasters